Curious George®

GROWS A GARDEN
A Double Reader

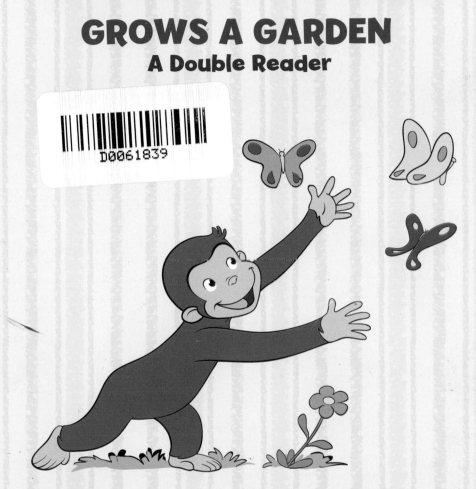

D0061839

Design by Joyce White
www.hmhco.com

ISBN 978-0-547-64304-5
Manufactured in China
SCP 10 9 8 7 6
4500715816

Houghton Mifflin Harcourt
Boston New York

Curious George®
Plants a Seed

Adaptation by Erica Zappy
Based on the TV series teleplay written by Sandra Willard

Jumpy Squirrel was very busy.

George was curious.

What was Jumpy doing?

Bill, the boy next door, told George,
"Jumpy buries acorns and nuts.
He stores them in the ground.

He can dig them up
later, when he is
hungry."

That gave George
a great idea!
George buried the orange juice.
He buried the butter.
He buried the bread.
He was glad to find a
good place to store food.

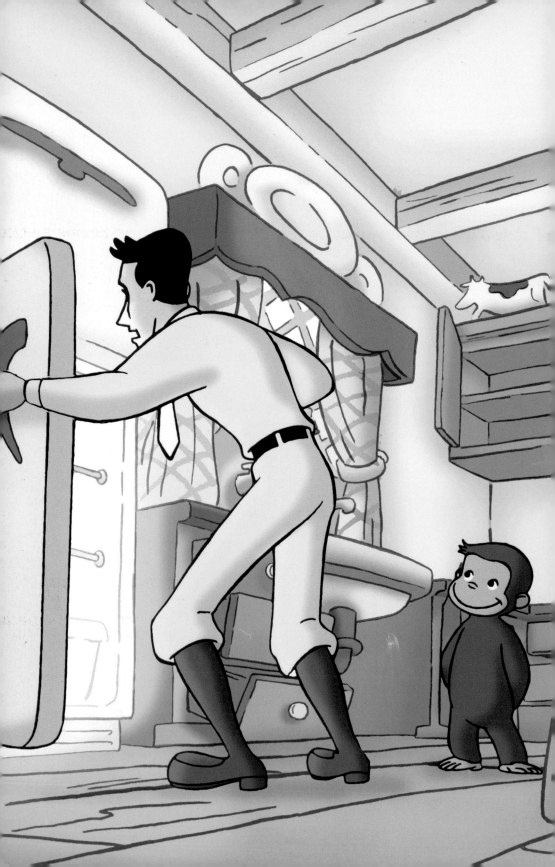

When the man with the yellow hat came home, the kitchen was empty! Where was all of their food?

George proudly showed his friend.

"George, orange juice and bread are not
for burying," the man with the yellow hat
said. "They cannot be stored in the
ground."

His friend showed George
a peanut with a sprout.
George was puzzled.

"This peanut grew into a plant,"
the man said. "Seeds and nuts
grow out of the ground, if they
are not eaten first."

George thought he understood.
If a little peanut could become a big
plant, what would a rubber band
become?

What would a feather become?

George dug lots
of holes.
He buried lots
of things.

Soon the house was empty.
The man with the yellow hat was
surprised!

"George, umbrellas and chairs are not for burying," the man with the yellow hat explained.

"They are made by people. They are not going to grow. Seeds and nuts will grow."

A few days later George saw
something new in the yard.
It was a sprout!
"Look, George," said his friend.
"A seed you buried is growing!
I wonder what it will be."

Soon there was a beautiful
sunflower in the yard.
George had a green
thumb after all!

You Can Do It

GEORGE DISCOVERS THAT NOT EVERYTHING GROWS . . . BUT SOME THINGS CERTAINLY DO!

If you'd like to grow something, try planting beans. In a few days, you'll have bean sprouts! You may need to ask a grownup for help with this exercise.

1. Fill a jar or plastic cup with half a cup of dried beans (a grownup can find these at the grocery store).

2. Cover them halfway with cool water.

3. Place a piece of nylon or cheesecloth on top of the cup and secure it with a rubber band.

4. Put it in a shady place for eight hours.

5. Gently drain the water through the cloth covering. Then add more water and immediately drain again.

6. Return the jar to the shady spot you found, but this time rest it on its side to give the beans more room to grow.

7. Rinse the beans twice a day for the next three days (as in step 5). After that, the sprouts will be ready to eat in a sandwich or salad! AND YOU GREW THEM YOURSELF!

Water Trail

If you'd like to know how water helps a plant grow strong, find a piece of celery and some food coloring — then you can see for yourself!

1. Ask a grownup to cut a single stalk of celery for you that still has the leaves attached to the top.

2. Pick a food coloring (red or blue works best) and add some drops of it to a full glass of water.

3. Put the celery, leaves at the top, in the glass of water and leave it in a sunny place.

4. In a few hours, you might notice something different about the celery. Wait overnight.

5. The next day, check out your celery. It will be colorful! Ask a grownup to cut the celery in half for you. You'll see colored dots inside the celery. This is how you know water travels from the bottom of the stalk up to the leaf—the same way it travels up the stem of a flower—to help the celery grow strong!

Show what color your celery stalk became.

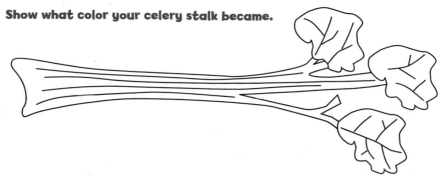

Curious George®
The Perfect Carrot

Adaptation by Marcy Goldberg Sacks
Based on the TV series teleplay written by Joe Fallon

Today was a special day.
George was helping Bill feed his bunnies.
The bunnies loved carrots.

George ran out of carrots.
Where could he get more?
Bill pulled a carrot from the ground!
George was curious.
"You can grow carrots too," Bill said.
"You just need carrot seeds."

The man with the yellow hat gave
George a packet of seeds.
They read the directions.

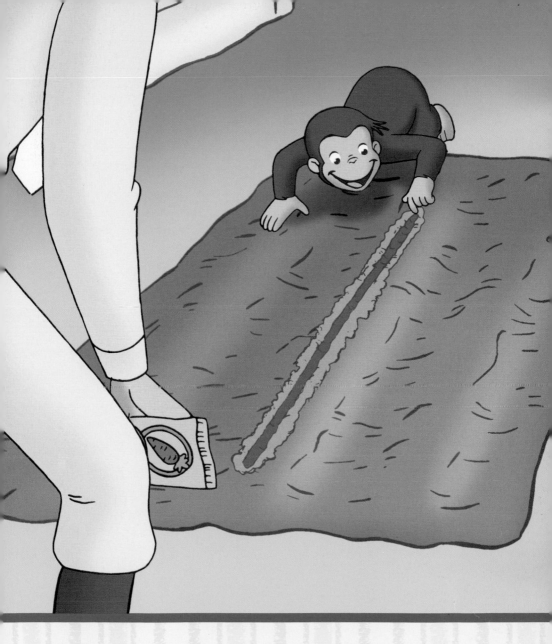

First, George dug a long hole in the ground.

Then he dropped
the seeds in one by one.
The man helped George cover the
seeds with dirt.

George watered them.
Dirt, water, and sunlight.
The seeds had everything they
needed to grow.

The next day there were no carrots.
George was confused.
"Carrots do not grow in one day,"
the man explained.
"Take good care of them every day.
They will grow in time."

George watered his carrots every day.
They started to grow.

George could not wait to see
his carrots.
He even dreamed about them.

After many weeks the carrots were ready.

George pulled them out of the ground.
Some of them looked funny.
But this one was perfect!

"Let's eat the carrot tonight!"
the man said.
But George wanted to save his carrot.
He put it in a case to keep it safe.

George went to show Bill his perfect
carrot. But Bill wasn't home.
A sign on the door said the bunnies
were missing!

George saw bunny footprints in
Bill's garden.
He followed them.

The footprints
led into a cave.
There were the bunnies!
They were lost and hungry.

George gave the bunnies his carrot.
While they ate, George went to
find Bill.

When they got
back to the cave,
the bunnies were still there.
But George's carrot was almost gone!

George did not mind.
His carrot was a hero—it had saved
the bunnies and the day!

Where Does Food Come From?

George grew fresh and delicious carrots right in his backyard. Did you know that a lot of the food we eat travels across the country in trucks, airplanes, and boats from very far away? A typical carrot has to travel more than 1,500 miles just to reach your dinner table!

Even if you can't grow your own vegetables like George, you can buy vegetables that are just as fresh and delicious from a local farm. Food you buy from a local farm is fresher, tastes better, and is healthier than food shipped long distances from other states or countries because the food doesn't spend days in trucks and stores losing nutrients.

Next time you go to the grocery store, see whether there is a sign for locally grown vegetables next to the other vegetables. Or ask an adult to find out if there is a farm near where you live. Call the farm to see when they're open and what they're selling. Many farms will schedule tours, and some even let you pick your own vegetables. Maybe you'll find a carrot as perfect as the one that George grew!

USDA Economic Research Service. "Farm Numbers/Largest Growing Fastest." *Agricultural Outlook*, October 2002.

Cooking with Carrots!

Did you know that you can cook delicious desserts with carrots? Ask an adult to help you with this yummy recipe for carrot muffins.

Here are the ingredients you will need:

1 ½ cups flour
2 teaspoons of cinnamon
1 ½ teaspoons of baking powder
½ teaspoon of baking soda
½ teaspoon of salt
3 medium eggs

¾ cup of granulated sugar
1 ½ cups of shredded carrots
½ cup of raisins or walnuts
½ cup of milk
½ cup of melted butter

Follow these steps:

1. Preheat your oven to 400° F.
2. Combine the flour, cinnamon, baking powder, baking soda, and salt.
3. In a separate bowl, beat together the eggs and the granulated sugar.
4. Add the shredded carrots, raisins or walnuts, milk, and butter; mix well.
5. Add the flour mixture and stir until the wet and dry ingredients are mixed completely.
6. Spoon the batter into twelve greased muffin cups.
7. Bake for 20 minutes.

Optional Frosting

Ingredients:

¼ cup of cream cheese, softened
1 tablespoon of melted butter
1 cup of powdered sugar
2 tablespoons of milk
½ teaspoon of vanilla

1. Mix together cream cheese and butter.
2. Stir in the powdered sugar, milk, and vanilla, and then drizzle over the top of the cooked muffins.